Home Edit Projects
Tips & Tricks to Edit Your House

Copyright © 2020

All rights reserved.

DEDICATION

The author and publisher have provided this e-book to you for your personal use only. You may not make this e-book publicly available in any way. Copyright infringement is against the law. If you believe the copy of this e-book you are reading infringes on the author's copyright, please notify the publisher at: https://us.macmillan.com/piracy

Contents

How to Organize Your Living Room 1

How to Organize Your Kitchen 11

How to Organize Your Bathroom 24

How to Organize Your Bedroom............33

How to Organize Your Playroom 39

How to Organize Your Living Room

1. Welcome the Wastebasket

If trash tends to accumulate in the family room, adding a wastebasket might cut down on clutter. Few family rooms actually have a wastebasket in them; they're not attractive and they can smell. Counteract this by choosing a can that fits your room's decor. If you know food will be thrown away here, get one with a lid and some deodorizing trash bags.

2. Keep Flat Surfaces Clutter-free

Papers, books, brochures and magazines tend to accumulate on flat surfaces all around the house, and the family room is no different. "You need a household information center, and the family room may be where that happens," says Julie Morgenstern, author of Organizing from the Inside Out. In fact, the family room is often more cluttered because it's a central gathering place in the house. A two drawer lateral file is Morgenstern's ideal recommendation - on average she says that's really how much paper it takes to run a home. If you don't have the floor space, a stackable file cart will do.

Make a quick sweep of all flat surfaces by piling papers in a bin, then sorting and purging as necessary. Take a vow, and get your family to follow it, to put papers in files rather than on the coffee table.

3. Control Out-of-Control Cords

Until the world goes wireless, we'll forever be stuck with tangled cables behind our entertainment centers. Fortunately, there are several options for taming cords in the family room. The most attractive is the slim Cableyoyo. It neatly coils up to six feet of cord and comes with an adhesive backing that sticks onto nearly any surface. A cable caddy usually sticks onto a desktop (or behind the TV console) and has a space for several cables to clamp into. Your cords will still dangle freely, however, so a cable zipper, which encloses all the cables in a tube, might be the best bet.

4. Create a Play Zone

If toys are taking over your family room, it's time to put them in timeout. Unused corners of a family room transform into great play areas because the walls serve to block encroaching clutter. Corners are also good areas to put a small bookcase or children's table. Add rolling bins for toy storage so your child doesn't have to feel confined, but is encouraged to pick up after he or she is done playing.

5. Coffee Table Functionality

If you have a coffee table (or forgot you had one due to the clutter) it's time to reassess its organizational capacity. Coffee tables that look great but don't have any storage for magazines, remote controls or even drink coasters, are probably making life more difficult. If you don't have the budget for a new one, consider adding low storage cubes, rolling baskets or bins to stick under the table.

6. Designate a Game Area

For a family that likes to play together, a game cabinet for board games and cards is both functional and fun. Games usually end up in a TV armoire, but it's helpful to designate a separate space for them, whether in another shelving unit, a bookcase or in plastic containers below the sofa (if the sofa has a skirt). Creating a single game space will free up other areas of the room for storage. If a computer is part of your gaming area, Julie Morgenstern recommends against a computer armoire. She's rarely seen them work well and recommends instead a desk that has a separate work surface, paper storage and a surface for the monitor.

7. Creatively Display Photos

If you have a lot of small, photo frames that tend to clutter your family room it's time to take control by displaying them in new ways. Photo albums and collage frames are great options for storing lots of photos at once, and a digital photo frame is especially handy for those who don't use film. Don't just use the mantel or side tables; use vertical space on the wall. Organizing your photos by date or occasion in photo boxes is especially helpful for scrapbookers, who can keep these in one central location on a bookshelf.

8. Take Advantage of Space Behind the Sofa

Organize extra blankets, pillows, candles in an accessible place - behind the sofa. It's a great place to put a trunk, cabinet or low bookcase. Plus, it gives you another surface to put a lamp or show off some treasured objects.

9. Sort Your Movie Collection

Multimedia like DVDs, videotapes and CDs are staples of the family room. Take 30 minutes to begin sorting your entire collection, making two piles: one for keeping and one for selling back or donating. If you no longer listen to the music or haven't seen the movie in ages (and don't plan on seeing it again), it's time to let go. There are plenty of options for storing your sorted collection: DVD towers, in a bookcase, ottoman or the drawers of a coffee table. Find a system that works for you.

10. Grow Your Houseplants

It can be a jungle in the family room if you have a green thumb. Organize your plants with a cute plant stand or several decorative pots. The type of houseplants you have will determine where you'll place them in the room, so keep that in mind when looking for a stand. Stands typically come in corner, pedestal and tiered configurations and some even have drawers so you can keep your fertilizer and watering can nearby.

11. Curb Your Collectible Enthusiasm

Collections, if you're not careful, can take over valuable storage space in a family room and can be even harder to organize. Large collections display best when bits and pieces are shown at a time (think shadow boxes) and rotated to keep the decor fresh. Cut your displayed collection in half by putting half of the pieces into an appropriately sized container and storing it in a hall closet. For added value, personal or otherwise, keep an inventory of each piece (date acquired, date of piece, description/significance) in the storage bin.

How to Organize Your Kitchen

The kitchen. Since it tends to be the hub of the household, every drawer and cabinet should be considered valuable real estate. Use it wisely to simplify your life and streamline your *entire* family's routine.

In a freezer, narrow bins and wire dividers keep items like frozen meat, bags of veggies, and boxed meals contained and easy to spot.

Nesting pots and pans on top of each other might *seem* like a space-saving solution but can make accessing them a nightmare from hell. Storing them upright between dividers makes it easy for you to grab what you need, and only what you need.

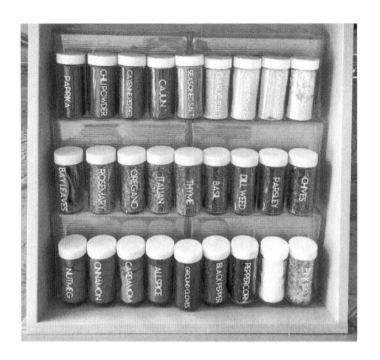

Storing spices in matching jars isn't purely aesthetics. The uniformity helps to maximize space, whether that's on a turntable or propped up in a drawer. For the finishing touch, add custom labels

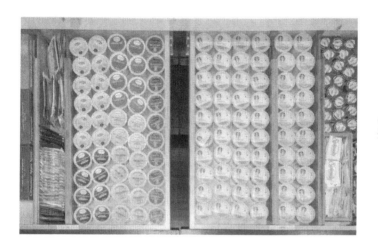

Keurig and Nespresso pods are the perfect size for drawer storage. Take advantage of every inch with expandable drawer dividers. This also works well for tea packets and creamers.

Too many dishes, not enough storage space? Look no further than risers to create a custom shelving solution without the help of a contractor.

Home Edit Projects

Who says the pantry is just for food? Take advantage of unused floor space with large bins for storing your back stock items, lunch boxes, etc.

Larger appliances can also be stored in the pantry to free up your kitchen cabinets and counters.

Deep kitchen drawers make the perfect snack station. Store your favorites in lidded canisters so they stay fresh and accessible.

Free up valuable drawer space by utilizing stackable bins (or shoe boxes!) for your seasonal table settings or party supplies and store in a cabinet you don't frequently access.

How to Organize Your Bathroom

1. Organize Your Medicine Cabinet

Make your medicine cabinet a repository of things you need and use regularly, which means chucking any outdated medicines and relocating excess to another location. "The way to achieve a clean countertop is to change the use of the medicine cabinet," says Julie Morgenstern, author of Organizing from the Inside Out. "They are better used for everyday grooming supplies rather than medicines."

Keep like items in their own labeled storage bins underneath the sink or in the linen closet. When you need to use something, slide the whole container out for easy access. You might choose to move medicines into the kitchen because moisture can ruin them. By creating "active" storage in your medicine cabinet you'll minimize time spent in the bathroom, giving you more time to organize another space in the house.

2. Control Hair Product Clutter

Gels, sprays, curlers, combs and hair dryers take up a lot of space in the bathroom. For quick organization, buy a plastic tub for under the sink and load it up with your supplies. As you place them in the tub, evaluate whether you use the product often. If not, donate it to a friend or to charity. When you fix your hair, the whole tub can be taken out and put away without creating a mess.

3. Add Creative Towel Storage

If your towel rack isn't big enough to hang the family's towels, add hooks to the bathroom. Towel hooks are inexpensive, easy to mount and create a space for each member of the family to hang their towel. No more fighting over whose is whose, plus your bathroom floor will remain dry, not damp.

4. Divide and Conquer Your Makeup

Drawers in the bathroom tend to be catchalls for lots of different containers, most of which badly organize their contents. An expandable cosmetic drawer organizer fits in a shallow drawer and takes the place of bulky cosmetic bags. Different size compartments will organize lipstick, blush and eye shadow so you never have to root around to find what you're looking for. As you organize your makeup, be sure to throw away anything that smells or is expired. Old makeup contains bacteria that can irritate your skin.

5. Reassess the Shower Caddy

It's your best friend when you're in the shower, but is it working for you? Shower caddies that are too small or too large can be a pain, both for cleaning you and your shower. There are plenty of options: from over the showerhead and suction shelves to corner caddies. If you don't have enough room, one solution is to pare down your toiletries. How many bottles of shampoo do you really need? If you have too much, consider downsizing so you don't feel like you have to fill up the extra space.

6. Claim the Space Over Your Toilet

Even in small bathrooms there's space for organization; you just have to know where to look. Over the toilet bath furniture is a great place to put extra toilet paper, toiletries and even towels. If you don't keep the toilet seat down, opt for a unit with cabinets or closed shelving. You can find attractive shelving at major home stores, usually for less than $100.

7. Add Style and Function With Apothecary Jars

If you have a lot of counter space, and don't mind leaving things out in the open, invest in some stylish apothecary jars to hold necessities. Cotton swabs, soap and bath salts look great in clear glass containers. These are especially handy when guests use your bathroom because they can help themselves without snooping in your cabinets.

How to Organize Your Bedroom

1. Use the space under your bed wisely.

Under the bed storage is great because it is not visible, but still very easily accessible. You can choose to store just a few items under there--I recommend things like gift wrap, or extra linens in an adult bedroom, and books in a children's bedroom--or you could be strategic and transfer the content of your dresser into rolling bin under the bed to free up space in your bedroom.

2. Artwork on walls!

Especially if you have a small bedroom, put your artwork on the wall and not on your dresser, nightstand, or vanity. Keep these spaces clear and your bedroom will have a more streamlined look.

3. Break the room down by major pieces of furniture and organize.

Organize the closet, under the bed (remember: always organize and declutter storage space first), dresser drawers, tops of dressers, night table drawers, tops of night tables, armoires, wardrobes, bookcases, etc.

4. Get your closet under control.

Even if your bedroom is spotless, if your closet is spirally out of control, it will disrupt the calm, serene state of the bedroom.

First things first, tidy up your closet, either by doing a full closet organization, or by doing a quick closet clutter sweep.

5. Consider a blanket rack.

If you have a ton of throws and quilts that you use regularly, and you have the floor space, consider a pretty blanket rack. This will make making the bed, and getting the bed ready at night ("turn down") easier. You won't be tempted to just throw everything on the floor.

The best place to find one is an antique or thrift store

6. Baskets for pillows.

Same goes for throw pillows. While men never do this, women--myself included--like to make the bed as comfortable as possible by employing as many throw pillows as possible. Use baskets to contain these while you're using the bed, stripping the bed and doing the wash.

7. Maintain a functional but clutter-free night table.

Rather than import a desk, choose a night table that suits your needs while taking up as little space as possible. A small dresser where you can store some clothing is a great space-saving trick that many professional organizers employ with clients who are living in tight quarters. if you don't have the room for a small dresser, try a slim night table with lots of drawers.

8. Make sure you have a hamper in your bedroom.

Either in the closet, next to the closet, or near the closet, a hamper will help clothes to stay in the closet and not spill out all over your bedroom.

You can choose one whose look fits your decor, or just use a basic hamper.

9. Finally, a garbage pail or trash bin.

Again, locate a small attractive garbage pail to keep in the bedroom. Look specifically for a pail because a big bin won't work, but you do need a spot to throw tissues, scraps of paper and all the other small pieces of trash that make their way into your bedroom.

How to Organize Your Playroom

Toys can be the worst, right? On one hand, they keep our kids entertained (which is helpful), but on the other, they have a way of completely taking over our homes without warning.

Thankfully, there are ways to control the chaos, in ways that kids can *actually* maintain. It doesn't matter whether you have a spacious playroom or just a corner in the living room, you can still create simple and intuitive systems that benefit the entire family.

Before we dive into this week's mini-projects, let's go over the basic principles of playroom organization:

-When purging items, NEVER ask a child if they still like something. They will *always* say yes, even if they've never touched it before. Just go with your gut.

-Create zones. Just like teachers do in a classroom. Kids thrive on routine, especially when cubbies and bins are involved.

–Don't get too specific with categories. There will always be an outlier and this will make sure everything has a definite home.

-Go label crazy. Once again, like in a classroom!

Designate a Drop Spot

Kids have a short attention span—it's unrealistic to think they will return a toy before grabbing another one. The solution? A designated drop spot, preferably with wheels. By containing the mess as they go, clean-up time feels much more manageable, especially when everything has a home.

Create a Colorful Displa

Install a set of low floating shelves to add a pop of color, free up floor space, and give kids easy access to their favorite books.

Many kids revere their completed Lego sets or large figurines as literal works of art, so you might as well use acrylic display cases to let them shine.

Bin Your Boxed Sets

Let's be honest, game and puzzle boxes aren't built for wear and tear. To preserve the items and avoid lost pieces, contain them separately in stackable bins that are durable and easier for little hands to grab.

Invest in An Elfa System

Home Edit Projects

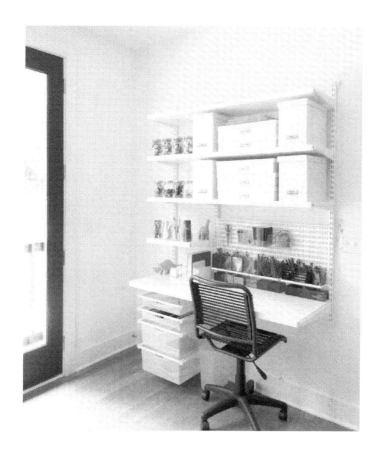

Contain by Size

Certain toys are easy to store while others are a bit more complicated. Either way, it all comes down to containing categories and providing easy access from playtime to clean-up time.

Create your own "parking lot" on a shelf for large vehicles. Not only will they be easier to access, it doubles as a fun and playful decor piece.

Contain smaller items like Legos, trucks, and figurines in stackable bins, sorted by color or type.

If you would rather utilize drawer space for smaller items, create a grab-and-go system with cups or inserts.

Home Edit Projects

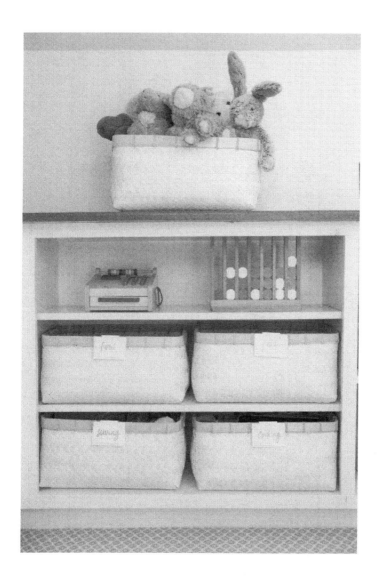

Choose cubby bins that are durable, roomy, and light enough for kids to pull from a shelf. We love minimal designs for concealing items, just make sure to add a labeled bin clip!

Since dolls come with *all* kinds of accessories these days, the categories can be a bit more specific. Store them in stackable bins, with the smaller items sub-divided in inserts.

Enforce Craft Control

Home Edit Projects

Turntables provide easy access to art supplies and can be sorted in ROYGBIV. It helps to include cups or jars in a turntable for items like crayons to keep them upright, making it easier to see every color.

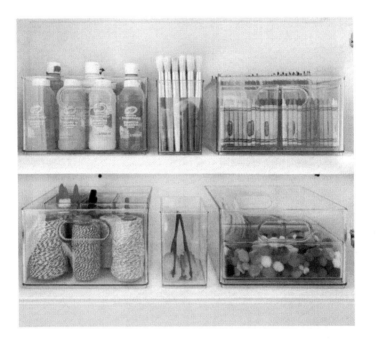

Use canisters and light bins to store supplies in separate categories, which makes it easy to remove only what you need from a shelf or cabinet and return it when they are done.

If you'd rather keep craft items hidden away (which we don't blame you), a 3-tier cart with categorized inserts is your solution. Wheel it out when it's necessary and store it away when it's not.

Made in the USA
Columbia, SC
30 June 2022